INVITATIONS

LYNNE ANN LEITE

SOUL STORIES PRESS

Invitations
Drawing Closer to God
A Poetry Devotional

Published by Soul Stories Press
Laguna Hills, CA, USA

ISBN: 979-8-9864481-0-7

Printed in the United States of America

This is dedicated to the One who invited *me*.
I am eternally grateful.

CONTENTS

YOU ARE
INVITED
TO DRAW
NEAR TO
GOD

Jesus

DRAW NEAR
TO GOD,
AND HE
WILL DRAW
NEAR TO
YOU.

JAMES 4:8

Introduction

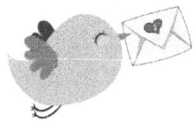

What is the most amazing invitation you ever received? Was it to a black-tie event with a guest list of famous attendees? Or maybe a special graduation ceremony. Perhaps you got an invitation to take part in an elite sporting event.

Once upon a time, I was invited to attend a Marine Corps ball. That was a pretty fancy affair. Women dressed in flashy evening gowns being waited on hand and foot by Marines decked out in their dress blues. It was impressive.

I can only imagine what it would be like to be invited to meet a member of royalty or get an invitation to a royal wedding. They would emboss the stationary with gold and include a royal emblem. The venue, a palace or cathedral of some sort, would be majestic. We would handpick sophisticated attire. Pomp and circumstance would rule the day and there would certainly be protocols for proper behavior around the royal family. Do not approach or talk without being asked. Bow or curtsy when introduced. And, whatever you do, do not touch the queen!

But that's my imagination for you, because an invitation from any member of the royal family, even the queen's dog, Candy, is inconceivable.

Do you know what seems really inconceivable? An invitation from the King of Kings, Jesus. And not just one invitation, but too many to count. And, yet, that is exactly what is happening every day. Jesus, the Creator of the Universe, is inviting us to draw near so we can know him better. His invitations are being delivered... the question is whether we will pause long enough to accept them.

It is my hope that this poetry devotional will help you do that. Writing it has been a labor of love that started with the first poem, *The Table*. As I was reading my Bible one day, I was struck by the image of a long table. I felt in my heart that Jesus was inviting us to that table, to join him, to fellowship with him. From that flowed the poem... and many others followed. It was soon very clear that each one centered on an invitation that Jesus is making to us. And that became this book.

It saddens me to think that many people won't accept his invitations. So I hope that one of these poems, in some small way, might speak to even one person, one soul, and encourage them to take that step of faith and RSVP a joyful yes to Jesus!

Each chapter starts with a poem followed by a short devotional and prayer. The next part of the chapter is your turn to meditate on how God is speaking to you. There are questions to consider and space to journal. There is no time limit or pressure to perform. The entire purpose of this little book is to help you draw closer to God - not cause you guilt or pressure. Start with chapter one, or start with any one title that captures your attention.

However, before you start, consider the most important invitation you will ever receive. Jesus is inviting you to be his child and become part of his family - and he sealed this invitation with his blood. So, if you have not yet accepted *this* invitation, then I encourage you to jump right on over to Chapter 16 now and start there. We can only draw closer to God the Father when we have accepted, through faith and grace, the sacrifice of his son, Jesus.

Are you ready to begin? If so, there are 15 invitations with your name on them just waiting for you!

YOU ARE INVITED TO THE KING'S TABLE

Jesus

AND THEY
SHALL COME
FROM EAST
AND WEST,
AND FROM
NORTH AND
SOUTH, AND
SHALL LIE
DOWN AT THE
TABLE IN THE
KINGDOM OF
GOD

LUKE 13:29

THE TABLE

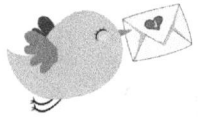

The family feud took a dark deadly turn.
His father, gone, never to return.

His body broken, no fault of his own.
His life so far removed from the throne.

A boy without hope, his fate, it seemed sealed.
An orphan with no chance to be healed.

Until the King invited him to dine
At his table, long, lavish, and fine.

The King showed him kindness, restored his life,
Never to live with longing and strife.

He's calling out to you to come as well.
Can you hear him ring the dinner bell?

All are invited to come and to dine
At a table long, lavish, and fine.

A more gracious Host will never be found.
At his table earth's treasures abound.

Though chaos and longing lurk at the door
Those at the table never need more.

Peace and plenty await those who recline
With him who is pure, holy, divine.

All are invited but not all will come.
Some hearts are hard and their minds are numb.

But all are invited to come and dine
At the table long, lavish, and fine.

With the One who is perfect, King of Kings,
Lord of all, Creator of all things.

He's calling you to dine: will you join in?
A place set for you right next to him.

A more gracious Host will never be found.
At his table all heaven abounds.

All are invited to come and to dine
At his table long, lavish, and fine.

♥

To learn more about Mephibosheth's story, the inspriation
for this poem, read 2 Samuel 4:4 and 2 Samuel 9:1-13.

THE TABLE DEVOTIONAL

Read 2 Samuel 4:4 and 2 Samuel 9:1-13

I love a good buffet. I'm thinking now of an all-you-can-eat lobster buffet where I have dined a time or two in the past. My mouth is watering just thinking about it! There was lobster bisque, lobster raviolis, lobster tails drenched in butter. But not only were there all things lobster to eat, this buffet included all kinds of other delicacies, including a dessert bar to die for!

> All are invited to come and to dine
>
> at His table long, lavish, and fine.

Truly, a trip to this buffet is culinary heaven. And yet it is nothing compared to the spread that waits for us in God's heaven. Mephibosheth got a taste of God's goodness while he lived on earth because he had a standing reservation at King David's table.

But it wasn't always that way. You see, Mephibosheth was the grandson of a king, but not King David. No, his grandfather was King Saul and a family feud between Saul and David left him crippled and orphaned, his royal lineage stripped away. He grew up a poor young man with no family and no way to support himself. Who would have thought this would be the life for the grandson of a king?

But then one day, King David asked of his aides, "Is there anyone left of the house of Saul to whom I may show kindness for Jonathan's sake?" And there was someone - Jonathan's son, Mephibosheth. Imagine what must have gone through Mephibosheth's mind when King David summoned him. "Oh, man, I knew it wouldn't last. I knew I'd be found out. Now I'm going to die. Time to pay for the sins of my grandfather."

Now imagine his astonishment when he hears instead, "Mephibosheth, my boy, I want to show kindness to you. Kindness like you've never known before. First, I'm going to restore your inheritance. Yup! You have a new pad right next to the palace. I want to keep you close so I can continue to show kindness to you. Every night there will be a chair for you, right next to me, at my table." Mephibosheth had heard about the king's table, and the banquets held there. The table overflowed with all the finest foods in the land. This was the invitation given to him? Truly a meal fit for a king!

The lobster buffet I've been to is a pricey affair - almost a hundred dollars a person. But from an earthly perspective, it's worth it. What about an invitation to sit at the King's table every night? Now that would seem priceless. But it isn't - it came at a dear cost. Jesus wants you and me to sit at his table and he paid the ultimate price for us to be there - he paid with his blood. God so desperately wants to show kindness to us that he sent Jesus to pay the price for us to sit at his table. All you have to do is accept the invitation. Will you be dining at the King's table?

❤

Dear Lord,
You are the bread of life. You promise that whoever comes to you will not go hungry and whoever believes in you will not thirst. You have prepared a table for us and you invite us, broken, sinful people, to dine with you. Thank you for this invitation that came with such a dear price. I thank you in the precious name of Jesus, the one who invites me. Amen.

QUESTIONS TO CONSIDER

What was the most amazing meal you ever ate? Was it only good food or was there good companionship, too? How does it make you feel to think about dining with Jesus?

Consider that the heavenly delights that await you will be infinitely greater than the earthly delights in front of you. Is that hard for you to imagine?

Has anyone ever treated you with extra kindness? Bought you a nice meal or gift or did something out of the ordinary for you? Maybe you were that person to someone else. How do you think our human kindness compares to God's kindness?

RSVP
take time to tell Jesus how you will respond to his invitation

YOU ARE
INVITED
TO THE
WEDDING

Jesus

BUT AS THEY
WENT AWAY TO
BUY, THE
BRIDEGROOM
CAME, AND
THE ONES
THAT WERE
READY WENT
IN WITH HIM
TO THE
WEDDING
FEAST, AND
THE DOOR WAS
SHUT.

MATTHEW 25:10

THE WEDDING

Where are you going? "A wedding," she said.
"The king and his bride are to be wed."

Hold on! Wait a second! I want to go!
I got an invite a while ago!

Give me a minute, the timings the worst.
There are many things I must do first.

She looked at her watch and said, "I can't wait."
I've longed for this day. I won't be late."

Stop, just a minute, I'll pare down my list.
If I'm not there, I know I'll be missed.

"I know that is true," she said, with a smile.
"He's longed for you for such a long while."

I went to prepare and when I looked back
The woman was gone, daylight turned black.

Where did the time go? There's much to do.
Saying good-bye to all that I knew.

Taking care of business - that can't be wrong.
Surely he'll wait. He's waited this long.

With invite in hand, I made the journey.
Knock! Knock! Knock! Lord, please open, it's me!

Inside I heard the wedding had begun.
The King and his bride. The Holy One.

With tears in my eyes, I once again read
His invitation written in red.

Dear one, you're invited, to wed with me,
To become part of my family.

I am the One, the Way, the King, the Groom,
You're the reason I rose from the tomb.

You must be ready, you won't know the day,
To leave all behind without delay.

Please prepare your heart now, don't hesitate
For on that day it will be too late.

You are invited, my love, to attend,
As souls are joined with me to the end.

Tears flowed from my eyes, a watery flood.
He signed his name with his precious blood.

To read the parable of the bridesmaids, the inspiration for
this poem, read Matthew 25:1-13.

THE WEDDING DEVOTIONAL

Read Matthew 25:1-13

It is truly unbelievable how much preparation goes into a wedding these days. I remember when I got married; it was so hectic and there was so much to do that I was late for my wedding rehearsal! That was over 40 years ago. Over time, wedding day expectations have only increased. I know this by seeing what was involved when my daughter and her husband prepared for their wedding, and my son and his bride prepared for theirs. It's overwhelming! So much to do, so many details and, inevitably, something will go wrong. In all the busyness and preparation, it feels like it could be easy to miss the heart parts of this important day. It's a life lesson you can only learn by living through it.

No wonder the Lord used a wedding as an example of what we can miss when we are too distracted, self-centered, or apathetic to stop what we are doing and be present. Even though Jesus is trying to get our attention, it's easy to miss the heart parts of our days.

He sends out the invite, "Come be with me. I'm having a wedding and I want you to be the guest of honor." How often do we drop everything to be present with him? I know, for myself, I often say, "I'll be right there, Lord, let me just finish this one thing. Yes, Lord, I will spend time with you in the morning." But then the morning comes and the dishes call, and work calls, and the bills call - and I can't hear Jesus calling even though I know he is.

Remember, I said I was late for my wedding rehearsal. At the time, I was a college student, and I had final exams two weeks before my wedding. I also worked part time, and so there wasn't much time to get the bridesmaids' gifts, and pick up the wedding band for my husband-to-be, and all the other last-minute details that needed to be attended to. So I was late. But, thankfully, neither the rehearsal nor the wedding could go on without me because, well, I was the bride.

Unfortunately, Jesus tells us that this won't be the case with his wedding. He has warned us in scripture that the day may come when it is too late and, even though he has invited us, we will miss the wedding. He is saying, "Come, join me." Yet we often respond, "Hold on, Lord, as soon as I find the perfect outfit, I'll be there." Or we think, I'll worry about getting prepared for the wedding tomorrow, not realizing the wedding is today.

> Please prepare your heart now, don't hesitate
>
> for on that day it will be too late.

Jesus says, "When I call you, come. When I invite you to be a part of my family, don't hesitate. In faith, accept my invitation. The wedding doors are open now but they won't always be." Won't you accept his invitation today?

♥

Dear Lord,
Remind me that this life here and all that keeps me busy, though blessings they may be, are all temporary. Convict my heart so I remember that there is nothing more important than you. I long to be at your wedding, so give me the power to focus on you and what matters most. I pray this in the precious name of Jesus, the one who invites me. Amen.

QUESTIONS TO CONSIDER

Have you ever said, "Hold on, Lord, let me finish this one thing and then I'll listen to you."? If so, did you ever feel conviction in your heart for putting off Jesus?

Can you think of a time when you missed an opportunity to do something God called you to do because you were too distracted by your own to-do list? How did that make you feel?

We have to live with the tension of an earthly life and things to do and God's desire for us to stay focused on heaven and Jesus' return. Can you think of ways to unite with Jesus in your heart and mind in the midst of this earthly life?

RSVP
take time to tell Jesus how you will respond to his invitation

YOU ARE
INVITED
TO TRUST

Jesus

BUT JESUS,
LOOKING ON
THEM, SAID TO
THEM, WITH
MEN THIS IS
IMPOSSIBLE;
BUT WITH GOD
ALL THINGS
ARE POSSIBLE.

MATTHEW 19:26

The Child

My child, my child, I have loved you since birth,
There is no greater treasure on earth.

My heart is broken to see you in pain,
Yet all I have tried has been in vain.

There must be a way for you to be well.
Wait! Is that the healer? Please do tell!

Healer, I called, I beg you, if you can,
make my child whole, oh please, Holy Man!

If you believe, all things are possible.
Do you believe that I am able?

I thought of my child, my heart filled with grief.
Lord, I believe, help me with my unbelief!

His eyes met mine and compassion I saw.
The love in his eyes filled me with awe.

Trust me with your doubt, your fears I relieve.
I know that your heart wants to believe.

I don't need much, faith like a mustard seed,
Becomes an oak when I take the lead.

I invite you to come, bring all your cares,
Bring me your heartache, give me your tears.

Trust me with your life, with the ones you love.
Believe that I have come from above.

All I ask is that you believe I Am
The Alpha, Omega, Lion, Lamb.

Dear one, come and see that your child is healed.
Believe in me and be Spirit sealed.

My child, my child, I loved you before birth,
There is no greater treasure on earth.

Read Mark 9:14-27 to learn about the man who inspired
this poem.

THE CHILD DEVOTIONAL

Read Mark 9:14-27

I have debated about getting a tattoo for several years. My family is divided about them and so I haven't gotten one... yet. If I got a tattoo, I would want one that says "believe" and I would get it on my inner wrist. For now, I have a bracelet that has "believe" stamped on it and I wear it with the word on the inside of my wrist. It is my version of a tattoo.

It's kind of embarrassing that I would want a tattoo that says believe. After all, I call myself a woman of faith and identify myself as a Jesus follower. I even share the good news with unbelievers. I feel ashamed that sometimes I need to be reminded to believe, to trust Jesus. And that is why I so resonate with this story in the Bible.

You see, this man, whose child is so broken, has a heart like mine. He desperately wants to believe and to trust, but he struggles. And with complete honesty, he cries out to Jesus - help me with my unbelief! If only he could see Jesus do a miracle, then he would believe and trust without hesitation. Wouldn't you? Of course, I'm sure that was the case when he saw Jesus restore his dear child to good health!

> Trust me with your doubt, your fears I relieve. I know that your heart wants to believe.

But we know from the Bible that many of Jesus' closest followers had trouble believing. And according to the Gospel of John, they saw so many miracles that you couldn't record them all in any book. These followers, too, must have cried out to Jesus - help us with our unbelief!

Can you hear my enormous sigh of relief? I know Jesus loved his disciples, despite their momentary and many lapses of faith. He didn't hold it against them. And if he could continue to love them in their struggle to believe, then he will continue to love me, and you.

In my soul, I believe. I believe Jesus is the only way to be saved, and that he loves me. But in the day to day of life, I struggle to trust. Not always. Just sometimes. Sometimes I struggle to believe and trust that God will protect my children and grandchildren from harm. I struggle to trust that he will provide when I see my bank balance dwindling. I struggle to believe good will conquer evil when I see what is going on in the world. Do you ever struggle this way? During those times, I thank God for the man in the crowd who was brave enough to cry out, "Lord, I do believe! Help me with my unbelief!"

Jesus invites us, during our momentary lapses of faith, to be authentic with him and to trust him, despite our unbelief. So I rub the engraved letters on my bracelet and I, too, cry out to the Lord, "I do believe! Lord, help me overcome my unbelief!" Will you accept his invitation to believe and trust him?

Dear Lord,
Thank you for inviting me to be authentic with you always. Thank you for your grace and mercy and love that never fails even when I struggle. Help me to believe and trust when my faith is weak. Forgive me when I doubt your love for me. I pray this in the precious name of Jesus, the one who invites me. Amen.

QUESTIONS TO CONSIDER

Is there an area of your life where you struggle to trust God? Family, finances, future? Is there something you can use, a verse or prayer card or piece of jewelry, to help you believe that God is trustworthy?

Does it comfort you to know that other mighty saints have struggled with unbelief at times?

Do you worry that if you call out to Jesus to help you with your unbelief that he will condemn you? If so, remember that he rewarded the father in the Bible for his authenticity. He desires that with you, too.

RSVP
take time to tell Jesus how you will respond to his invitation

YOU ARE
INVITED
TO BE
AMAZED

Jesus

SEE YOU AMONG
THE NATIONS,
AND BEHOLD,
AND WONDER
MARVELLOUSLY;
FOR I WORK A
WORK IN YOUR
DAYS, WHICH
YOU WILL NOT
BELIEVE,
THOUGH IT BE
DECLARED TO
YOU.

HABAKKUK 1:5

THE UNEXPECTED

The man had possessions and position.
He had power and recognition.

With all that he had, one thing he had not:
Skin that was clear of spot after spot.

"My love," said his wife, "how are you today?"
"Sad," he said, "from being pushed away.

If the damage to my skin weren't enough,
The way people look at me is tough."

A young girl who helped his wife with their house
Said, "I know someone to treat your spouse."

The man, who was desperate, went on his way,
To find the person without delay.

He took with him an elite team of men;
But was this wishful thinking again?

He looked with fear at his festering skin
And thought, is this a fight I can win?

By now they found the house of the prophet.
The man, prepared, pulled out his wallet.

But the prophet didn't come out at all.
Instead came his aid with a cure-all.

"Go and wash seven times in the river.
Skin that is clear, this will deliver."

The man felt his face flush hot with anger.
"I came all this way to meet this stranger!

Why can't he come out and speak to my face?
Call on his Lord and ask for his grace?

I came all this way so I could hear this?
We're going home," he said with a hiss.

"Don't go," said a man on his elite team,
"Because you expected a grand scheme.

Yes, this is simple, so what would you lose
To do as he says. Sir, please don't refuse."

They went to the river. Seven times in.
And the man came out with perfect skin.

He went to the prophet with gift in hand.
"There is no God like yours in the land.

Wonders he does in ways least expected.
In him alone am I perfected."

The prophet said, "I will not take a thing,
For only my Lord I serve as King."

"And I, too, will serve him," the man replied.
"Inside my heart His word will I hide.

His invitation I have accepted.
He is God of the unexpected."

To learn more about Naaman, the inspiration for this
poem, read 2 Kings 5:1-21.

THE UNEXPECTED DEVOTIONAL

Read 2 Kings 5:1-21

Maybe you've heard this one, but maybe not. There was a man who was stranded on a deserted island. He cried out to God to rescue him. Not long after, a ship sailed by and the captain called out to him, "Do you need help?" He called back, "No, I'm waiting for God to rescue me." A little while after that, a helicopter circled overhead. "We're here to rescue you," the pilot said. "No, that's okay," the man said. "I'm waiting for God to rescue me." Days went by and then weeks and finally the man cried out to God, "Lord, why aren't you rescuing me?" And God replied, "Son, first I sent a ship, but you wouldn't go. Then I sent a helicopter and you still wouldn't go. What do you expect me to do?"

That's a good question, isn't it? What do we expect God to do? Have you ever had a situation where you expected God to respond and act in a certain way and he responded differently? I sure have. More than once. Sometimes God comes through with trumpets blaring, and his response to the situation is so unbelievable it feels like a miracle. Other times, his response is as quiet and gentle as a feather floating to the ground. Sometimes our own expectations keep us from even seeing what he is doing in our lives, amazing things that only the creator of the universe could do. And we miss it because it's not how we thought it should be.

If that describes some of your experiences, as it does mine, don't feel bad. Naaman experienced the same thing, and God still shared his story in the Bible. Naaman had tried everything to rid himself of leprosy, an insufferable disease, to no avail. The God of the Hebrews was his last ditch effort.

How often do we do that? Make God our last ditch effort after trying all human options to solve our problems. "Well, I guess now all we can do is pray." Yikes!

When Naaman finds out how God wants to heal him, he is mad and wants to go home. This was not a solution he saw fit for his situation! Does any of this sound familiar to you? It does to me. Thanks anyway, helicopter pilot, keep going. I have an expectation of how God is going to respond to my situation, and this isn't it, so move on. I'll continue to stay here in my misery, thank you.

Eventually, Naaman does as he is told, and God healed him. God's way turned out to be much more amazing than his own. This changes his life, but not only in a physical sense but also in a spiritual one. God invited Naaman in to see him work in an unexpected and amazing way. And maybe because it was unexpected, it caused Naaman to have a deeper faith than he would have had otherwise. Jesus is inviting you to be amazed by the unexpected. Will you accept his invitation?

His invitation I have accepted.

He is the God of the unexpected.

Dear Lord,
Help me to remember that your ways are not my ways, that your solutions to my problems are often unexpected to me but never a surprise to you. Please give me the awareness to see you at work and prepare me to be amazed. I pray this in the precious name of Jesus, the one who invites me. Amen.

QUESTIONS TO CONSIDER

Have you ever prayed for a change in a situation or a person and God answered your prayer in a way you didn't expect?

Has God ever amazed you by going above and beyond what you expected during a time of need in your life? How did this affect your faith?

Is God inviting you to trust him to provide you with a solution to a problem you currently have or rescue from a situation? Is it hard for you to go to God first rather than as a last resort? If so, why do you think so?

RSVP
take time to tell Jesus how you will respond to his invitation

YOU ARE
INVITED
TO BE MY
FRIEND

Jesus

BEHOLD, I STAND AT THE DOOR, AND KNOCK: IF ANY MAN HEAR MY VOICE, AND OPEN THE DOOR, I WILL COME IN TO HIM, AND WILL SUP WITH HIM, AND HE WITH ME.

REVELATION 3:20

THE TAX COLLECTOR

Friend, why are you looking so down and out?
Oh, you're the tax man? That's it, no doubt.

What a terrible job! Hated by all!
Never invited. Never a call.

Have you heard about this Friend of sinners?
He attends tax collector dinners.

Oh, and he takes a beating for it, too.
The leaders are livid through and through.

That doesn't stop the Son of Man, Jesus.
Maybe you heard about Zaccheaus?

A very wealthy tax collector is he,
Who decided he would climb a tree

To see the one called the Son of Man.
But this Jesus had another plan.

"Zacchaeus," he said, "come on down from there.
I have dinner plans. Do you know where?

Your house, tonight, with you and all your friends."
Zacchaeus, overjoyed, made amends.

"Half of what I have, I'll give to the poor.
I'll change my ways for you, my Savior."

The crowd muttered about the planned dinner.
"He goes to the house of a sinner!"

Jesus, undeterred, enjoyed his entree
And then to Zacchaeus he did say,

"Don't worry about this proclamation
For to your house has come salvation.

I have come to seek and to save the lost.
And I will do it at any cost."

My friend, do you like the story I told?
Your spirits seem lifted sevenfold.

But wait, there's more that I have to tell you!
Did you hear of the tax man Matthew?

Jesus told him, leave all and follow me.
He obeyed and Jesus set him free.

Then to Matthew's house they went for dinner.
The crowd cried, "Look! Friend of a sinner!"

"I come to call sinners to repentance,"
Jesus said to all in his presence.

"It is not the righteous I come to call,
But those who are broken by the fall."

Friend, it doesn't matter your vocation,
Jesus is the way to salvation.

It doesn't matter the choices you've made,
If you repent, your debt will be paid.

Friend of tax collectors and sinners, too,
He came to die for me and for you.

When Jesus calls and invites you to dine,
Drop everything and with him recline.

♥

To learn more about Zacchaeus' story, read Luke 19:1-10
and for Matthew's story, read Mark 9:9-13.

THE TAX COLLECTOR DEVOTIONAL

Read Luke 19:1-10

Have you ever felt like a social outcast? Or been in a situation where you felt like you didn't belong? For me, two words come to mind. High. School. High school was a pretty cliquish place when I attended. Was it for you?

> Friend of tax collectors and sinners, too,
>
> He came to die for me and for you.

We had all kinds of groups. There were jocks, loadies, brainiacs, low riders, surfers, the popular kids, the goodie-two-shoes, and I'm sure several more that I can't remember. Personally, I never felt like I belonged to any of them.

The cliquish nature of my high school wasn't, and isn't, unique. How do I know? Because it's part of our human nature. Read through the Bible and you will see that the in-crowd and outcasts have been around since the beginning of mankind. They certainly existed during the time Jesus walked on earth. People with leprosy—outcasts. What a sad situation. Through no fault of their own, people ousted them from their community because they had a very visible, very contagious disease.

And then there were the tax collectors. Another set of outcasts, but ones who contributed to their negative social situation. The tax collectors were Jewish men hired by the Roman government to collect taxes from their fellow Jews. The Roman taxes were many and burdensome, and many tax collectors would inflate the amount a Jewish citizen owed and then they would pocket the difference. No wonder their community cast them out!

But Jesus, too, was an outcast. The in-crowd at the time were the pharisees, the leaders of the Jewish community, and they hated Jesus. He was a threat to everything they held dear - power, prestige, possessions. They bad mouthed him constantly and the consequences for associating yourself with Jesus was to lose privileges within your community.

Jesus, the outcast. No wonder he healed the lepers and reached out to the tax collectors. He understands what it feels like to not be part of the in-crowd. The sad realization is that we are all outcasts - outcasts from the God who created us because of our sinful condition. But Jesus, friend of sinners, came to earth to live a perfect life, die on the cross, and rise from the dead, all so we could become part of God's in-crowd. And he offers that invitation to everyone.

Have you ever felt down and out because the in-crowd didn't include you? Or worse, have friends, your community, or even your family cast you out? Jesus understands, he cares, and he is calling you to be his friend, to be part of his crowd. Will you accept his invitation?

❤

Dear Lord,
You became an outcast to save an outcast like me. Thank you for all you have done for me. Your love is overwhelming! Help me to remember this always. I pray this in the precious name of Jesus, the one who invites me. Amen.

QUESTIONS TO CONSIDER

When was the last time you felt like an outcast? Does it help to know that Jesus, too, was an outcast?

In Luke 18:9-14 Jesus tells a parable about a humble tax collector who understood he was a sinner in need of a savior. When did you first really come to realilze that you were in need of a savior?

Have you ever felt the need to pray for someone or a group of people who were outcasts? What led you to pray for them?

RSVP
take time to tell Jesus how you will respond
to his invitation

YOU ARE
INVITED
TO
FOLLOW

Jesus

AND HE SAYS TO
THEM, COME
AFTER ME, AND I
WILL MAKE YOU
FISHERS OF MEN.

MATTHEW 4:19

THE FISHERMAN

The trade of my people was good to me.
Fishermen all filled my family tree.

My father a fisherman, brother, too.
Fishing was all I knew how to do.

Day after day we would get out our nets.
Life on the sea, as sweet as it gets.

Nothing else for me. I'll fish till I die.
Then he spoke to me as he walked by.

People were saying that he was the One.
He did things that had never been done.

What is that you said? Be part of your crew?
But fishing was all I ever knew!

I'm not a priest, minister, or pastor!
What can I do to serve the Master?

Come, follow me, and be fishers of men.
What if he doesn't ask me again?

At once I left my nets to heed his call,
Committing to him once and for all.

Trusting in faith he would show me the way.
Following him each and every day.

My family tree is now filled with those
Who left all behind because they chose

To follow him and be part of his trade
Fishing for souls whose debt he has paid.

♥

In the Bible, three gospel accounts tell us about how Peter, the inspiration for this poem, became a follower of Jesus. You can read those accounts in John 1:35-42, Matthew 4:18-22, Mark 1:16-20.

THE FISHERMAN DEVOTIONAL

Read Matthew 4:18-22

Have you ever had a job you didn't feel qualified to do? To be honest, I sort of felt that way when I became a grandmother! Even though I had successfully fed, clothed, and raised two children to adulthood, I felt like a complete newbie when my first granddaughter was born.

It seems like every time I have started a new job or career, I felt inadequate. There's never been a time that I walked into a job feeling overqualified, like I could do the job in my sleep. For me, there has always been some sort of learning curve. Then once I've been at it for a while, it all becomes second nature and I forget that I ever felt unqualified... except maybe being a grandmother!

The thing is, we get comfortable once the learning is done, and the skill mastered. Even if we are stuck in a dead-end situation, it is much easier to keep doing what we're doing than change. So what happens when it is Jesus inviting us to make a change?

Maybe he sees you are stuck in an unfulfilling career and he is encouraging you to follow him to something better. Perhaps you have the potential to make more money than you currently are, but fear or feelings of unworthiness prevent you from making a change, even though God is waiting to bless you in this way. Many things can keep us stuck where we are or keep us returning to what we know.

But if God calls you to something new, he will equip you for it. If he is saying drop your nets and follow me, then he has a plan for you. I know it's hard. It is super hard for me. And I'm confident it was hard for Peter, because later in scripture, when Peter is down and out, we see him returning to what he knew - his fishing boat.

Even if Jesus is not calling you to change your life situation - your work or where you live or what church you attend or anything else - he is still inviting you to follow him. And that may be the scariest thing of all. Because following Jesus isn't just about those types of life decisions - following Jesus means being his testimony wherever you are and whatever you are doing. Jesus wasn't calling Peter away from being a fisherman; he wanted Peter to also be a fisher of *men*. He invites us to do the same.

And if you think you are not qualified to do this because you don't have an education in theology, or you are an introvert, or you think you have to quit what you are doing to work full time in ministry, you are wrong. As I said, if Jesus calls you, he will equip you. I didn't think

> Trusting in faith He would show me the way.
>
> Following Him each and every day.

I was qualified to be a godly grandparent, but Jesus is equipping me day by day. When Jesus invites you to follow him, will you go?

❤

Dear Lord,
Sometimes I am afraid to follow you, afraid to leave what is comfortable and known. But I want my life to be a living testimony. Please equip me to do your will and give me the faith and courage to go where you lead. I pray this in the name of Jesus, the one who invites me. Amen.

QUESTIONS TO CONSIDER

Can you think of a time when you chose a path that felt safe and secure instead of the path Jesus may have been calling you to take? How do you feel about that decision now?

What does being a fisher of men and women look like to you? Do you believe that if Jesus calls you he will equip you? Remind yourself of the truth that he will!

Do you feel Jesus is inviting you to follow him outside your comfort zone? What does that look like?

RSVP
take time to tell Jesus how you will respond to his invitation

YOU ARE
INVITED
TO BE
KNOWN

Jesus

COME, SEE A MAN
WHO HAS TOLD
ME ALL THINGS I
HAD EVER DONE:
IS NOT HE THE
CHRIST?

JOHN 4:29

THE WATER

She heard the whispers from behind and knew
That their words about her were all true.

She told them, "I'll get the water, you stay."
Grateful for the chance to get away.

The movie of her past played in her mind
As she walked along, she hit rewind.

Every failed marriage, and there were many.
Oh, guilt and regrets! She had plenty.

The gossipers had much to talk about
And it left her feeling down and out.

Deep in her thoughts, completely unaware,
She didn't notice him sitting there.

"Hey there," he said, "will you give me a drink?"
"Me?" she said, not knowing what to think.

"Don't you know who I am? Why talk to me?"
She lowered her eyes. "Please let me be."

"I know all about you," he said with a smile
"I've had my eyes on you for a while.

From before you were born, I knew your name.
All that you've done, I love you the same."

She studied his face and said, "Who are you?"
"I am all that is lovely and true,

The living water you are thirsty for.
Won't you let me give you that and more?

Let me wash you clean with holy water
To live for me and things that matter.

Believe in me, don't wait when I call,
Let me be your husband, your all in all."

"Could You be the One? My Savior? My Lord?"
"I am He. Go and believe my Word."

She went back to her friends, family, and town
But this time she wore a royal crown.

He rewrote her story, script, and movie,
And now she had a testimony.

All came from near and far to hear her tell
About the man she met at the well.

The Holy King who made her his daughter.
The One who gave her living water.

Read about the woman at the well in John 4:1-42.

THE WATER DEVOTIONAL

Read John 4:1-42

If you could write the script to your life story, what would it be? A Hallmark romance? An action adventure? A comedy? Regardless of the genre, you, as the hero in your story, would certainly shine. Not a single blemish or wrinkle on your face when the camera zooms in. In every scene, you would save the day. All the unpleasant parts would wind up on the cutting room floor, edited out. The director, megaphone to his mouth, would shout, "All right, people, let's get this in one take. And let's make Lynne look perfect." Yup, that's how I would want it. I'm laughing right now! That is so Hollywood... and life is, well, not Hollywood.

There is only One who led a perfect life, one perfect story. The rest of us have stories that are flawed, broken, damaged. Sometimes they get that way because of our own bad choices and sometimes the result of the bad choices of others. Sometimes our stories have rough parts simply because our DNA strands were damaged from the brokenness of our ancestors.

> He rewrote her story, script, and movie,
>
> and now she had a testimony.

Have you ever watched a movie that includes gratuitous violence or sex? You know it when you see it. It's a scene that has no function in the story other than to excite and arouse the emotions of the viewer. I dislike that. Alot. That's lazy and cheap storytelling, if you ask me. But these particular scriptwriters, they don't ask me. And they definitely don't ask God. Because that's not how God writes a script.

Yes, many of our stories include very painful parts, many scenes we would like to cut out; but if we allow God to be our scriptwriter, those scenes will never be gratuitous. He

THE WATER DEVOTIONAL   63

will use even the saddest parts of our story for good. No film is wasted with God. Nothing ends up on the cutting room floor. If we invite him to be the author of our story, he will redeem even the most painful of scenes. Only he can turn a character from a zero into a hero.

And that's how it was for the woman at the well. Even though we don't know her name, we know her story. And it was salacious. A result, it sounds like, of bad choices on her part and bad choices by others who hurt her. Her story evoked judgment and exclusion from those around her. So imagine her surprise when a man, from a community at odds with her own, treats her with such gentleness and kindness. The Scriptwriter who knows every scene in her life up to that point and still offers forgiveness and hope for a happily ever after ending... if she will only accept his invitation to drink the living water he is offering her. It chokes me up just to think about it.

That is his invitation to you and to me - to rewrite our stories with a heavenly pen. Will you accept his invitation?

Dear Lord,
Thank you for being the author of life and for taking the painful parts of my story and redeeming it. Thank you for giving me the opportunity to accept, by faith, the gift of living water that you offer and for the blessed assurance of an eternally happily ever after with you in heaven. I thank you in the precious name of Jesus, the one who invites me. Amen.

QUESTIONS TO CONSIDER

Is it hard to believe that God can use even the difficult and painful parts of your story for good? If so remember, with God all things are possible.

Do you ever have a hard time forgiving yourself for some of the choices that have affected your story? Remember God has said that he is faithful and just to forgive our sins.

Can you think of a time in your life when God used a painful part of your story to bless someone else? Take a minute to thank him for turning what was meant for evil to good.

RSVP
take time to tell Jesus how you will respond
to his invitation

YOU ARE
INVITED
TO
DECIDE

Jesus

BUT AS FOR ME
AND MY HOUSE,
WE WILL SERVE
THE LORD.

JOSHUA 24:15

The Wall

She gazed out from where she sat on the wall.
The kingdom beyond made her feel small.

On the other side, a city within,
A painful reminder of her sin.

How long could she sit, one leg in, one out?
And then she saw the enemy scout.

Not one, but two, and they wanted to hide
Inside her home – now time to decide.

She heard of their God who did mighty things
And filled with fear the hearts of the kings.

She wanted to worship a God like theirs
Who would wipe away all of her tears

And forgive her for the places she'd been,
Give her the chance to be born again.

I will hide you, she firmly decided,
But your protection must be provided.

Not only for me, but my family, too,
For I know a battle will ensue.

Not only for the kingdoms of the earth
But for souls who are of greater worth.

There is only One good enough to save
Sinful souls from an eternal grave.

It's time to decide, to answer his call.
No longer will I straddle the wall.

As for me and my house, the Lord we'll serve
And trust in him our souls to preserve.

To read Rahab's story, the inspiration for this poem, read
Joshua 2:1-21.

THE WALL DEVOTIONAL

Read Joshua 2:1-21

"Forty and single again? Good luck with that! You have a better chance of getting struck by lightning than finding love again..." My colleague's words droned on, but I stopped listening. I was still trying to process what was worse - being single for the rest of my life or getting struck by lightning.

As a newly separated woman, my insecurities were higher than the wall that guarded Jericho. I had married before I was 20 and knew nothing of dating as an adult, middle-aged woman. Was she right? Would no one ever love me again?

From the top of my wall of insecurities, I looked out to the world. I wanted validation from the world that I was worthy of being loved again. I wanted men to find me attractive and funny. Some friends said I should do what made me feel good. After all, you do only live once. Sure, I wasn't divorced yet, but divorces can take a long time and I was already 40. Apparently, I didn't have much time left, so I ventured off the wall into the world of dating.

But inside my heart a battle was brewing. Like Rahab, I had a choice to make. Because during this painful time in my life, I had found love. But not the love of man. I found the love of Jesus.

And so I went back to straddling the wall - on one side were the affirmations of man and all the world offered, and on the other side was Jesus with an invitation.

"Lynne," I could hear Jesus say, "let my love be enough. Let me provide you with security."

I wish I could tell you I immediately jumped off the wall into the arms of Jesus and every insecurity and fear I had vanished. I jumped off the wall and accepted Jesus' invitation. And I put my dating life on hold. Still, I struggled with insecurities and fears. But I never regretted getting off the wall. Only in Jesus did I find my true worth and forgiveness for all the bad choices I had made. I even found peace in tumultuous times.

> It's time to decide, to answer His call.
>
> No longer will I straddle the wall.

In the end, what my colleague said was wrong. She didn't know what Jesus did - that I would be married in my forties because my husband and I eventually reconciled. Jesus restored our marriage when we accepted his invitation and decided to live in and for his kingdom. Now, when you come to our house, you will see a tapestry that hangs prominently in our living room. It is a colorful, peaceful scene with these words woven into the tapestry, "As for me and my house, we will serve the Lord." Jesus is inviting you to decide which kingdom you will serve. Will you accept his invitation to choose his kingdom over the world?

Dear Lord,
Sometimes the world's ways are so inviting and I am tempted to do things, not according to your will, but according to my desires. Please forgive me for those times when I have chosen the world over you. Help me to firmly plant my mind, heart, and feet in the truth of your word. Help me, every day, to choose to serve you. I pray this in the precious name of Jesus, the one who invites me. Amen.

QUESTIONS TO CONSIDER

Can you think of a time when you said "yes" to something even though God said "no"? How did that make you feel? Always remember, when you repent, God is always faithful and just to forgive.

Is there anything keeping you from accepting Jesus' invitation to be all in for his kingdom? If so, what is it? Ask Jesus to help you let it go.

If you have already made a committment to be all in for Jesus, how does that make you feel? Excited? Scared? Blessed? Deprived? Consider your emotions, both positive and negative, and remembr that God can handle your negative emotions.

RSVP
take time to tell Jesus how you will respond to his invitation

YOU ARE
INVITED TO
LIVE AN
ADVENTURE

Jesus

I AM COME THAT
THEY MIGHT
HAVE LIFE, AND
MIGHT HAVE IT
ABUNDANTLY.

JOHN 10:10

THE BUSH

Who would think this would be his life story.
He started off in royal glory.

An adopted son, not royal by birth,
Left riches behind for greater worth.

A lifetime had passed, or that's how it felt.
Almost eighty years under his belt.

A family man and a shepherd by trade,
Too old now for new plans to be made.

Then one day as he watched over his flock
Something amazing – he looked in shock.

There where he stood on the mountain of God
A burning bush did not burn – how odd!

He turned to step closer to see the sight.
A voice from the bush gave him a fright.

"Moses, you're on holy ground," the Lord said.
The word of the Lord made him stop dead.

He took off his shoes and covered his face,
In awe of God, Moses knew his place.

"Moses, I have something for you to do.
I've seen my people and what they've been through

I hear their cries and I will set them free
Into a land of milk and honey.

And you, Moses, will help me make it so.
I'm sending you to Pharaoh, now go."

Who me? Moses thought. I'm way past my prime.
He's mistaken. He'll realize in time.

A million excuses went through his mind.
"Lord, there must be someone else you can find.

I am old, unskilled, and slow of speech.
What you ask is far beyond my reach."

"Moses, as you shepherd a helpless lamb,
So I go with you, the great I AM.

To be part of my mission to rescue
Is my personal invite to you."

No more excuses for turning away
Moses knew there was no more to say.

And so his greatest adventure began
When he decided to be God's man.

Miracles happen when we're in his hands,
Cause age doesn't matter in God's plans.

For when we choose to be his precious lamb,
We adventure with the great I Am.

♥

To read how Moses' great adventure with God began, read
Exodus chapter 3.

THE BUSH DEVOTIONAL

Read Exodus Chapter 3

The idea of starting a podcast had been noodling around in my brain for several years. I had even taken a class at our community college to learn more about radio and what it was like to be an on-air host. I read books, bought some equipment, and in particular, I listened to another podcaster who taught people how to start a podcast.

Then I got the email. The subject line read, "Anyone can start a podcast. Even 60-year-old Dr. Barbara." *Even 60-year-old Dr. Barbara?* I was approaching the 6-0 decade - was that so old that the 30-something-year-old sender of the email found it amazing that even a 60-year-old can start a podcast? I began to doubt myself.

Then we entered the season of the Coronavirus pandemic. My daughter, bless her heart, kept reminding my husband and me to be extra careful. Don't forget your masks. Maybe think about using two. Are you stocked up on hand sanitizer? After all, and here was the gut jab, you are in a high-risk age bracket. I was feeling my age... maybe older. I suddenly felt the urge to become a greeter at Walmart and to eat my dinner while I watched Wheel of Fortune and Jeopardy.

> Miracles happen when we're in His hands,
>
> cause age doesn't matter in God's plans.

But on a more serious note, I wondered if I was wasting my time with wanting to start a podcast and the writing and speaking I was doing. It felt like I had missed my chance to do all that I felt God had called me to do. After all, I was now in the season of grandparenting.

I have taken this question, and doubt, to the Lord many times. And each time I have felt him say to me, "You are still there, Lynne! I do have things for you to do. Dreams to fulfill for you. Trust me."

That is why Moses' story is so meaningful to me. And John's, whose story included writing the book of Revelation at an old age. What about Anna and Simeon? Both were octogenarians when they testified about Jesus. On the other side of the spectrum is Joseph's story, a young man who prophesied and managed a nation's resources. And David, a young shepherd destined to be a king. Plus, everyone in between.

Age is a human construct. Sure, our bodies go through changes as it travels through time. (Oh, how I wish I could reverse some of those changes!) But God doesn't look at a person's age - old or young - he looks at a person's life and their willingness to live it for him regardless of the number attached to them. Moment by moment, in every season of life, Jesus invites us to dream, to plan according to his will, to do and to create and to live with purpose.

As long as we are here, he will have something for us to do. And, occasionally, if we are willing, he will invite us to do something spectacular for his kingdom, like he did with Moses. Will you say yes when he invites you?

Dear Lord,
Age truly is just a number to you. Thank you for allowing me to dream and to serve you in every season of life. Please empower me to do both. I pray this in the precious name of Jesus, the one who invites me. Amen.

QUESTIONS TO CONSIDER

Can you think of a time when you felt too old or too young, too weak or inexperienced, for the task you were called to do? Were you able to complete the task? If so, how? If not, why do you think you were unable?

Looking back, do you now believe God had a purpose in having you be the one to fulfill that task or mission?

Can you think of a task or mission God may have for you to do in your current season of life? What is it? Is there anything keeping you from accepting Jesus' invitation to join him in his work? What can you do to remove that obstacle?

RSVP
take time to tell Jesus how you will respond to his invitation

YOU ARE
INVITED TO
WORK WITH
ME

Jesus

WHATEVER YOU
DO, WORK
HEARTILY, AS FOR
THE LORD AND
NOT FOR MEN.

COLOSSIANS 3:23

The Picnic

"Where are you going?" my mom asked that day.
"To hear all that the Prophet will say."

"Will you be back home for the midday meal?"
"No, I want to hear all he'll reveal."

"Well then, let me pack you something to eat."
I thanked her and set off down the street.

I joined a crowd of people, long and wide,
Following him up the mountainside.

As people walked by, I heard them exclaim,
"Who is this man who can heal the lame?"

"I saw him heal a man who was born blind."
"There is none like him in all mankind."

I wondered, as I listened to them chat,
If I would see him do things like that.

Not likely, I thought, with so many here.
What are the chances I can get near?

The sea of people, too many to count,
Pushed me up to the top of the mount.

That's when I saw him, his face like the sun.
No wonder they say he is the One.

Being in his presence put me at ease.
Love flowed from him like a gentle breeze.

As I watched him, he sat down on the ground.
Friends and followers gathered around.

"Let us buy food for these people," he said.
"We don't have money for that much bread!"

His friends were shocked, confused by his request.
They didn't know that this was a test.

I looked at the lunch bag still in my hand.
Some bread and fish weren't all that grand.

But then I thought, maybe now I will see
Something amazing happen to me.

To one of his friends I said, "Take my food."
He sighed, "Not much for this multitude."

He gave it to the Prophet nonetheless
And the Prophet held it up to bless.

I watched as he took what little I gave
And fed the people, wave after wave.

Each one ate until they were satisfied.
Baskets of leftovers stupefied.

Five loaves. Two fish. How was that possible?
Only because of a miracle.

From the beginning, I'm sure that he knew
Exactly what he had planned to do.

He invited me to give him that day
All I had – his power to display.

Not only a prophet - my Creator,
A miracle worker - my Savior.

Up close and personal he came to me
To give me life and to set me free.

This poem was inspired by one line in scripture, John 6:8 and wondering what it must have been like for that boy, whose fish and bread, by the power of Jesus, fed more than 5,000 people. You can read the account of feeding the 5,000 in all four gospel accounts: John 6:1-15, Matthew 14:13-21, Mark 6:30-44 and Luke 9:10-17.

THE PICNIC DEVOTIONAL

Read John 6:1-15

A dear friend of ours was getting ready to make the long journey to Rwanda... again. He had been there many times working on a ministry project to help encourage entrepreneurship within one particular community. The purpose of the mission was to open a coffee shop which would serve as the learning grounds (like I how I did that?) for running a small business. It would also be a gathering place for people in the area where they could, hopefully, learn about Jesus.

It cost our friend a lot, in time, talent, and especially treasure, to travel from California to Rwanda and, for this trip, he was short of the funds he needed... by a lot. Not only was there the cost of travel, but he needed many supplies to get the coffee shop up and running.

"I wish there were more we could do," I remember my husband saying. At this time in our lives, we felt blessed that we could make a decent donation; but he was still very short of what he needed. Then I had an idea.

"What if we did one of those matching things? Like we hear other ministries doing?" I asked. "We could match donations, dollar for dollar. If that works, he would have what he needs." So we ran the idea by our friend and he was excited, and grateful, to try it. He put the word out on social media and in no time he had what he needed, and more, for his trip and for his mission.

Jesus wasn't standing there, miraculously doubling our dollars, the way he did when he multiplied the fish and bread. Nonetheless, he took our meager offering and multiplied it to meet a need. In our times, we rarely get to see, up close and personal, the kind of supernatural miracles Jesus did when he walked the earth. But we can still see him at work, magnifying what we give him. Jesus still does miracles today, and he still uses ordinary people, like you and me and the boy with the bag lunch, to accomplish his purposes.

Sometimes we can see the miracle unfold, as with our friend's ministry needs. Sometimes we won't see what Jesus did with what we gave him until a later date. Maybe not even until we get to heaven. What an exciting time that could be... if we will offer what we have clasped in our hands to Jesus to use for a miracle. *If.*

> He invited me
> to give Him
> that day
>
> all that I had –
> His power to
> display.

Imagine if the little boy had listened to his growling stomach instead of hearing the need around him. Imagine what would have happened if he had worried about what his mother would think about him giving away the costly food she had prepared for him. Imagine what would have happened if he thought, "What can Jesus possibly do with my couple of fish and bread? I feel ridiculous even offering it." What is Jesus inviting you to give him? Just imagine what he can do with it when you do!

♥

Dear Lord,
Help me to live each day ready to give you whatever is in my hands to use for your glory. Remind me that, in your hands, what little I have can be miraculously made into so much more. I pray this in the precious name of Jesus, the one who invites me. Amen.

QUESTIONS TO CONSIDER

Can you think of a time when Jesus took something you had and turned it into so much more?

Have you ever witnessed Jesus do a miracle? Could Jesus be inviting you to be someone's miracle today?

Were you ever surprised to find out something you did that you thought was insignificant turned out to be important?

RSVP
take time to tell Jesus how you will respond to his invitation

YOU ARE
INVITED
TO MY
VICTORY

Jesus

BUT THANKS TO
GOD, WHO GIVES
US THE VICTORY
THROUGH OUR
LORD JESUS
CHRIST.

1 CORINTHIANS 15:57

THE BATTLE

All were invited to come and to see,
A battle destined for victory.

The people were called from all walks of life,
To a mountain venue set for strife.

One side brought many, boasting of might.
He stood alone in the morning light.

Come, said the man, bring all that you've got.
The people watched as the day got hot.

They called to their gods as hours wore on
That for them the battle would be won.

But no power there, it was all in vain.
The man standing alone spoke again.

Stand back and watch, said the man to the crowd,
My God will prove worthy, he avowed.

Fire from heaven devoured the wood
The people, in shock, silently stood.

Why do you waver between two choices?
Time to decide, lift up your voices.

Fire from heaven now burned in their souls
And praises to God did they extol.

All are invited to come and to choose.
Battle lines drawn, there's no time to lose.

Why do you waver between two choices?
Time to decide, lift up your voices.

Live in a world of chaos and strife
Or sign your name in the book of life.

One Man stood alone, the way, truth and light,
He is the one who will win the fight.

All are invited to come and to be
Alongside him in his victory.

───────────────❤───────────────

The inspiration for this poem is the story of the battle at
Mount Carmel. You can read about it in 1 Kings 18:19-46.

THE BATTLE DEVOTIONAL

Read 1 Kings 18:19-46 and 1 John 5:3-5

People like to take sides. Sports is a perfect example of this mysterious aspect of the human condition. And it isn't a recent phenomenon. After all, the Olympics started over 2,000 years ago.

It's fascinating, at least to me, to see the way and the lengths to which people will go to associate themselves with a sports team. There's the clothing, the team flags, and all the team accessories. There are Super Bowl parties with attendees fiercely cheering on "their" team in between bites of guacamole laden chips. The association with a team is serious, and emotional, business. Just watch the students sitting in the stands at a major college football game sometime and see how many cry when their team loses. I get it. I can be an all-in fan sometimes, too.

> All are invited to come and to be
>
> Alongside Him in His victory.

But it isn't just sports that cause people to take sides - it also permeates into other aspects of our lives. It seems like today, more than ever, we are called to pick a side. Are you a conservative or liberal? Vaccinated or unvaccinated? Meat-eater or vegetarian? Paper bags or plastic?

Okay, I admit, that last one was pretty inconsequential. But when you really think about it, most of the things we align ourselves with in life are. The stakes are much higher when the side you choose involves the fate of a human life. Send in troops to battle or not. Admit you are a Christian and die or denounce your faith and live.

But the most consequential alignment we will make is spiritual. There is a spiritual battle raging all around us and

God is asking us, no, he is demanding us, to take sides. It's an alignment that affects not only our time here on earth, but how we will spend eternity. Nothing less than our souls are at stake. The battle lines are drawn, and the outcome has already been determined. All that's left is to decide - whose side will we be on?

If this were a Super Bowl game and you knew the final score ahead of time, would you gather as much money as you could and bet on the winner? It seems like an obvious decision. If you did, it could set you up for life!

In the spiritual battle, Jesus has told us the final score ahead of time. Only one side will be victorious - his. Choosing his side means being set for *eternity*!

Jesus is inviting us to lift up our voices louder than the most ardent football fan. Faced with opposition from the world, he is inviting us to stand firm for his ways and his truth. And most importantly, he is inviting us to stand alongside him in victory. Will you accept his invitation?

♥

Dear Lord,
In this divided world I am often called to take sides. Help me to remember that the most important decision I will ever make is to align myself with you. Give me the power to stand firm for you and your truths even in the face of fierce opposition. Thank you for saving me in this spiritual battle so I can stand with you in victory in heaven one day. I pray this in the precious name of Jesus, the one who invites me. Amen.

QUESTIONS TO CONSIDER

Can you think of a time when you were called to take sides? How did that make you feel?

Is God calling you now to take that step of faith and choose to stand with him on a specific issue or just in your day to day life?

The Apostle Paul uses the metaphor of Jesus followers as soldiers. What does it mean to you to be a part of God's army?

RSVP
take time to tell Jesus how you will respond
to his invitation

YOU ARE
INVITED
TO RUN
FREE

Jesus

IF THE SON
THEREFORE
SHALL MAKE YOU
FREE, YOU SHALL
BE FREE INDEED.

JOHN 8:36

THE RACE

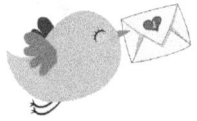

I approached the start, energy to spare.
The race began strong without a care.

Surrounded by people, ready to run,
Don't compare, this is a race of one.

Besides, am I not young and on fire?
Doing all the Lord will require?

The first leg of the race started with ease.
A peaceful street lined with olive trees.

Flat as flat could be, no hills before me.
I ran along feeling so carefree.

Until I turned a corner and saw it,
A hill, no a mountain, I admit.

How is this here? Where did everyone go?
And suddenly I felt my pace slow.

Someone from the side said, "You're over pal!"
It hit hard and lowered my morale.

Still up I went as sweat poured from my brow.
Another jeer, "How ya doin' now?"

Over and over many attacks came
And my enemy knew me by name.

Who said it was supposed to be this hard?
I could feel myself becoming scarred.

Doubt, fear, anger, envy, consuming me.
Weighted down, I would never run free.

Sad and all alone now to run my race,
Until I saw Jesus face to face.

Persevere, my child, you are not alone.
I am with you even from my throne.

And a cloud of witnesses cheers you on.
Look now, your accusers are all gone.

"I'm sorry Lord!" I cried, "Forgive my sin!
I race for you, Lord! I want to win!"

With him at my side, my focus shifted,
The shackles loosened and weight lifted.

Keeping my eyes on all that is holy
I could run the race set before me.

I don't race alone, he's there by my side,
My coach, my trainer, my perfect guide.

Each step that passes the end is in sight
And I know I have fought the good fight.

You have kept the faith, I want him to say,
Each and every hard step of the way.

And one day soon I will finish the race
Because of his unwavering grace.

To hear, my desire is so fervent,
Well done my good and faithful servant.

This poem was inspired by several verses in the Bible. Here are a few: Hebrews 12:1, Matthew 25:23, Hebrews 13:5.

THE RACE DEVOTIONAL

Read 1 Corinthians 9:24-27

Have you ever been in a race before? Maybe a marathon. Is that too much? How about a 5K? Still too much? How about a wheelbarrow race? It seems like races have changed little since the time Jesus was on earth. I'm sure our training methods and foot attire are different, but as Paul told the Corinthians, we run to get a prize. Or at least he is telling us we should.

At age 50, with no prior experience and very little athletic ability, I ran a half-marathon. Okay, ran is an exaggeration. It was more like fast walking, with some jogging sprinkled in. Even with my daughter as my coach and my partner in the race, it was hard. There were many mile markers along the way where I thought my race would end.

But I persevered. I wanted the prize. Half-marathons are not like 5-year-old soccer leagues - everyone does not get a participation ribbon. If you are too slow, in fact, they will pick you up and drive you to the finish line. No one wants that. Thankfully, I could cross the finish line on my own two feet and get that fancy bling called a race medal.

I can't imagine trying to complete that course while wearing a weight vest or ankle weights. Or without training for weeks ahead of time. And it would have been foolish, if not dangerous, to do it without coaching before and during the race.

Our life here on earth is more than a physical journey from birth to death - it is a spiritual journey as well. And the apostle Paul compares it to what God knew would be a universal human experience - a race.

How can we do well in our spiritual race if we do not rely on a Coach to guide us and encourage us? How can we run with the added weight of sin, guilt, and shame? How can we stay on course when distracted by shortcuts and donut shops? Okay, maybe I was the only one distracted by donut shops!

Persevere, my child, you are not alone.

I am with you even from my throne.

Jesus is inviting us to let him be our coach. He is pleading with us to give up the weight of sin by turning away from it and toward him. At every mile marker, he gives us the strength and power to continue. He is the one, along with a cloud of witnesses, cheering us on to complete our race.

At the end of the half-marathon, when I crossed the finish line, I heard my name over the loudspeaker. One day I want to hear my name over heaven's loudspeaker with the added words, "Well done, Lynne, my good and faithful servant." Don't you? And the bling you get at the end of this race is far better than any medal - it's a heavenly crown. Jesus is inviting you to race with him. Will you accept his invitation?

Dear Lord,
Help me to remember that I am never running my race alone. You are running right alongside me every minute of my race. Lord, give me your power and strength to run well. Thank you for welcoming me with open arms at the finish line. I pray this in the precious name of Jesus, the one who invites me. Amen.

QUESTIONS TO CONSIDER

Do you ever feel like you are running your race alone? Consider that Jesus said, "Lo, I am with you always, even unto the end of the world." How does this truth make you feel?

Is there anything that is weighing you down? Unrepentant sin? Shame or guilt? Take a moment to confess it to Jesus and let him set you free.

How does it make you feel to know that there is a cloud of witnesses cheering you on so that one day you will hear Jesus say, "Well done, good and faithful servant."

RSVP
take time to tell Jesus how you will respond to his invitation

YOU ARE
INVITED
TO SIT
WITH ME

Jesus

AND SHE HAD A
SISTER NAMED
MARY, WHO
ALSO, HAVING
SAT DOWN AT
THE FEET OF
JESUS WAS
LISTENING TO HIS
WORD.

LUKE 10:39

THE JAR

As the beautiful fragrance filled the room
I sensed my friends beginning to fume.

Why this waste? They asked with indignation.
That didn't stop my adoration.

This wasn't the first time I caused upset.
There's the dinner Martha won't forget.

I didn't mean to make my sister mad
But being near him made me so glad.

I sat at his feet, she fussed with dinner,
But his food satisfies the sinner.

Martha, Martha, he said, why do you fret?
Being with me, Mary won't regret.

His presence was all I longed to pursue.
There was nothing better I could do.

He alone holds the keys to life and death.
When someone dies, he can give them breath.

I witnessed this firsthand and know it's so.
When my brother died, he came to show

His mercy and love and power so great.
Although I thought he got there too late.

Still, when I saw him, I fell to his feet,
Oh, to believe death he could defeat!

Moved with compassion, that's just what he did.
Because of his words, my brother lived.

And that is why on that fateful evening
As I sensed he soon would be leaving

I gladly broke my alabaster jar
My most valued possession, by far.

Not caring what the others thought of me
I knew what it cost to set me free.

I poured out the oil, the scent filled the air
I knelt and washed his feet with my hair.

The smell of the perfume was bittersweet
As I worshiped my Lord at his feet.

To learn more about Mary's story, the inspiration for this
poem, read Luke 10:38-42, John 11:1-45, and John 12:1-8.

THE JAR DEVOTIONAL

Read Luke 10:38-42

If I asked you to give something to someone, you would have three options. You could give them your time, talent, or treasure. Those are your options. If I'm being honest, I would have to say that I prefer to give my treasure. It's so much easier, don't you think? Write a check and mail it to a worthy ministry. Slip a couple of bucks to the person sitting outside the grocery store raising money for homeless people. Have you done that? I have. And when I do, I stand a little taller. How about you?

Yes, I enjoy giving from my treasure because time is, well, since we are being honest, so limited. And talent? That's risky. I might face rejection if I give out of my talent. But no one has ever rejected my check or my cash.

Of course, the check I write will not leave my bank account balance at zero. And I don't give all the cash in my wallet because that would be foolish. What if I need some for an emergency? Like coffee? Hmmm... I'm noticing that I am not standing quite so tall.

> His presence was all I longed to pursue.
>
> There was nothing better I could do.

It's difficult, isn't it? To give someone your all. But that is what Jesus is inviting us to do - to give him our time, talent, and treasure. Mary accepted this invitation and Jesus said she had chosen the good portion. Jesus said that her sacrifice of time, talent, and treasure, which others criticized, would cause her story to be shared right along with the gospel. Wow!

Jesus isn't asking us to give him our all because he needs it, but because he loves us. It's an invitation. We don't have to accept it. We can continue on with our to-do list and preparations and complain, like Martha, that if we didn't have all this work to do, we would happily sit at the feet of Jesus.

We can continue to hide our talent under a basket out of fear that others might reject us. We can continue to give out of our excess. And do you want to know something? Jesus will still love us just as much. But, as he told Martha, we would miss out on the good portion. I don't want to miss out on that – do you?

Mary gave all because she understood that all had been given for her. Jesus gave his all so that her sins could be forgiven. Jesus gave his all so that her story, which some say was shameful, could be rewritten. Jesus gave his all so that she could sit at his feet, not only here on earth, but one day in heaven. And Jesus did the same for you, and for me. He is inviting us to give up all and sit at his feet. Will you accept his invitation?

❤

Dear Lord,
Help me to pause in my busy life and accept your invitation to sit with you and to listen to you speak. You gave all for me because you love me so much. Help me to use all you have given me, my time, talent, and treasure to bring you the glory you deserve. Let me love you as the woman with the alabaster jar loved you - extravagantly. I pray this in the precious name of Jesus, the one who invites me. Amen.

QUESTIONS TO CONSIDER

Which do you find hardest to part with: your time, talent, or treasure? Why do you think that is?

Can you think of a time, or times, when you related more to Martha than Mary? How did that make you feel?

What are some ways you can be more intentional about sitting at the feet of Jesus?

RSVP
take time to tell Jesus how you will respond to his invitation

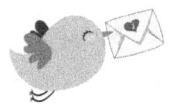

YOU ARE
INVITED
TO GET
OUT OF THE
BOAT

♡

Jesus

FOR GOD HAS
NOT GIVEN US
THE SPIRIT OF
FEAR, BUT OF
POWER, AND OF
LOVE, AND OF A
SOUND MIND.

2 TIMOTHY 1:7

THE BOAT

To him, the boat was a safe place to be,
Protecting him from the changing sea.

Many a storm he had weathered aboard,
Tucked in the stern till calm was restored.

Inside felt secure, outside there were threats.
Stay in the boat with the safety nets.

If he needed food, the boat would provide,
If protection, a good place to hide.

When he was confused, he knew where to go
To find comfort when life dealt a blow.

Inside felt secure, outside there were threats.
Stay in the boat with the safety nets.

Then Jesus came and said, Come follow me.
Leave your boat and your security.

I came to give life in all its fullness.
Follow me and live in my goodness.

You can walk on water with eyes on me,
Jesus said as he stood on the sea.

Don't be so afraid, get out of the boat.
Look at me, I will keep you afloat.

I know that you're scared, you think all is lost,
Following me has come with a cost.

You want to run back to what you have known,
Your life on the boat, your comfort zone.

But that is not the life I have for you,
Forgiveness, fullness, to start anew.

The thief comes to steal, but I come to give
The life that I have for you to live.

He saw Jesus standing there on the shore
And jumped from the boat, he wanted more.

Jesus, his eternal security,
His safety net in life's stormy sea.

Read John chapter 21 and Matthew 14:22-33 for the
inspiration for this poem.

THE BOAT DEVOTIONAL

Read Matthew 14:22-33

Have you ever struggled with anxiety? Or, worse yet, had a panic attack? I remember the first time I had a panic attack. It went something like this:

Me: Doctor, I'm having a heart attack! Doctor: No, Lynne, I'm certain it is only a panic attack. Me: Clearly you don't know what you are doing. Where did you go to medical school? On the Internet? When I die and my children are left without a mother, that will be on you. Doctor: Let me give you a sedative for now. But please go see your primary physician to follow up regarding the panic attack.

That was the abbreviated version and, to be honest, some of that may have been internal thoughts and not spoken out loud. But I'm sure you can get the idea. That was the beginning of a very dark and challenging season for me.

I'll never know for sure why panic hit. I always felt like I could handle so much in my life. Me, the ultimate plate spinner. So having panic attacks confused me. There was probably a physiological component, since several close family members also struggled with anxiety disorders. And I couldn't deny that my broken emotions contributed to the problem.

My struggles with anxiety and panic attacks have ebbed and flowed over the years. Some seasons of life have, thankfully, been panic free while others have been life altering. In those times when the panic was at its most intense, I could feel my comfort zone shrink. I didn't want to leave my house for fear of having a panic attack some place that didn't feel safe. Driving became a challenge. My home and immediate family members became my safety nets.

I have sought all kinds of help, like medication and counseling, with varying degrees of success. Certainly, I have cried out to the Lord to remove my anxiety completely. That hasn't happened. But I have managed, and in most circumstances, my comfort zone is pretty wide these days.

Not that I don't still struggle - I do. I am a work in progress. Thankfully, Jesus continues to call me out of the boat. He extends his hand and invites me to take ever so tiny baby steps to stretch my comfort zone. And if I have a bad day, or week, or season, he doesn't treat me the way I treat myself. He doesn't pile on condemnation. He patiently sits in the boat and waits until the right time to invite me out again.

Yes, like Peter, I know a thing or two about nets, safety nets, that is. Jesus tells us that, in this world, we will have trouble, but we can be encouraged, knowing that he has overcome the world. Ultimately, he is the only safety net we need, and he is inviting us to step out of the boat and trust him. Will you accept his invitation?

> Don't be so afraid, get out of the boat.
>
> Look at me, I will keep you afloat.

♥

Dear Lord,
You tell us that in this world we will have trouble. When the storms of life rock my boat, remind me that you are my safety net. Fill my heart with the truth that you love me even when I struggle to trust you. Empower me to grow my comfort zone. I pray this in the precious name of Jesus, the one who invites me. Amen.

QUESTIONS TO CONSIDER

How do you feel when Jesus calls you to step outside your comfort zone - do you jump right into the deep end, or do you dip your toe in the shallow end?

Was there a time in your life when you felt confined by your own fears?

When you have chosen to play it safe and stay in the boat, have you suffered from self-condemnation? What do you think Jesus would say to you instead?

RSVP
take time to tell Jesus how you will respond to his invitation

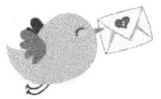

YOU ARE
INVITED
TO BELIEVE

Jesus

FOR GOD SO
LOVED THE
WORLD, THAT HE
GAVE HIS ONLY
BEGOTTEN SON,
THAT
WHOSOEVER
BELIEVES ON HIM
MAY NOT PERISH,
BUT HAVE
ETERNAL LIFE.

JOHN 3:16

THE TOMB

"He's gone!" the women burst into the room.
"The Lord's body is not in the tomb!"

The apostles were still deep in their grief,
But two followed them in disbelief.

To the tomb they went, not sure what they'd see.
The women were right – it was empty.

"Why look for the living among the dead?
That's what the angel told us," they said.

The men went back home, not sure what to do.
One woman stayed - her heart broke in two.

She wept because she wanted to believe.
But him alive she couldn't conceive.

He is risen, the angel had told her.
Someone stood nearby - a gardener?

"Why are you crying there?" she heard him say.
"Someone has taken my Lord away."

"Mary," he said, and she instantly knew
That what she'd been told really was true.

"Rabboni!" she cried. "My source of delight!"
"I told you I would make all things right.

Now go tell the others no more to grieve.
I invite you simply to believe."

"I do!" she replied and set off to share
The good news entrusted to her care.

"Disciples," she said, "I have seen the Lord!
He is alive! He has been restored!

Peter, a fresh start you have been given.
Thomas, touch where the nails were driven."

Only he has power over the grave.
Only he has the power to save.

Blessed are those who believe and never see.
Stop doubting and believe it can be.

Yes, the tomb is empty because he lives!
He loves and he heals and he forgives!

In heaven with him for eternity –
We live because the tomb is empty.

♥

The inspiration for this poem is the empty tomb and
resurrection of Jesus! The accounts are in all four gospels:
Matthew 28, Mark 16, Luke 24, John 20.

THE TOMB DEVOTIONAL

Read John 20:24-31

My husband lovingly, and sometimes not so lovingly, calls me Missouri. It's kind of like a nickname, but one he only uses when I am doubting something he says or perhaps something I have heard or read. Our exchange often goes something like this:

"The temperature today is supposed to get to 106 degrees," says hubby. "Oh, come on, that can't be right. I'm not sure I believe that," I say. "Okay, Missouri, check it out for yourself."

As long as I can remember, I've heard the phrase that Missouri was the "show me" state and I understood the reference to mean that people from Missouri might generally be a skeptical group.

If Missouri had been a state in 33 A.D., I think there might have been a conversation among the disciples of Jesus that went something like this:

"The tomb is empty!" says Peter. "Jesus talked to me!" says Mary. "He rose from the dead!" says John. "Yeah, right. I'll believe it when I see it," says Thomas. "Okay, Missouri, put your fingers where the nails were and put your hand in my side," says Jesus.

Then Jesus says, "Stop doubting and believe."

> Blessed are those who believe and never see.
>
> Stop doubting and believe it can be.

Some people believe without needing to fact check or research. Someone told them, maybe as a child, you are a sinner. Okay, they think, that's easy to believe. I know that's true. You need a Savior. Well, if I'm a sinner, then that must be true. Jesus, the Son of God and God Himself, came to earth and died to save you from your sins. Whew! Thank you, Jesus! I believe!

Of course, I might be oversimplifying the process somewhat, but I know people who take God at his word with no need to examine the evidence for the truth of the gospel. Maybe that's why Jesus said whoever does not receive the kingdom of God like a child shall not enter it.

I believed in Jesus as a child, but as I became an adult, I was confronted with an unbelieving world. Was what I believed as a child true? The Missouri in me came out. I studied the scriptures and looked at the historical evidence to back up what is written in the Bible. When I finished asking God to show me and doing my research, I concluded that, even though I may not understand it all, the Bible as written is true, historical, spiritual, and mysterious.

Here's the thing - we will never see perfectly and know everything with certainty in this human body. There will always be a certain amount of mystery, if there weren't, then we would be God. In this world we cannot say, "Jesus, show me the nail holes and the wound in your side." That's why he told Thomas, "You believe because you have seen. Blessed are those who can't see but still believe." Those people Jesus is referring to is us.

But there is enough evidence, even for this show me gal, to believe that Jesus is the Son of God who came to earth to die for all the bad things I had done. And if I believe this and ask him to forgive me for all that I have done to hurt him, then he is just to forgive me. If, by faith, I ask Jesus to be my Savior, then he promises to save me from an eternity apart from him - he promises to prepare a place for me in heaven. And the same is true for you.

Jesus offers a simple invitation - though you can't see me, believe. It's a matter of life and death, so do what you need to do to put aside your skepticism and simply believe.

♥

But these are written, that you might believe that Jesus is the Christ, the Son of God, and that believing you might have life through His name. John 20:31

PRAYER

Have you accepted Jesus as your personal Lord and Savior? If not, are you ready now to accept his invitation to believe? He loves you and he is just waiting for you to make that decision! Accepting Jesus as your Lord and Savior doesn't require any special training. It doesn't require you to be living a perfect, or even good, life. You don't need to make special arrangements with a church leader.

All that is required is that you believe. Believe that you have done things in your life that have hurt others or offended God. Understand that you will never be good enough, on your own, to spend eternity with a perfect and Holy God. Acknowledge that Jesus, who is fully God and fully man, came to earth to die for all the bad things you have done. Believe that he died on a cross, was buried in a tomb, and after three days, God brought him back to life. Believe that by dying on the cross, he took the punishment for your wrongdoing, your sins. When you believe in him and accept his sacrifice for you, you can be forgiven and become a child of God. Believe.

One way we acknowledge our belief in Jesus to save us from our sins is through prayer. Prayer is not about fancy words or something you have memorized, prayer is simply talking to God and telling him the desires of your heart. A simple prayer follows, a prayer similar to the one I prayed when I accepted Jesus as my Lord and Savior. If you are ready to take that step of faith and put your life in the hands of Jesus, then I encourage you to pray this prayer.

♥

Dear Lord Jesus,

I do believe you are the Son of God and that you died on the cross to pay the penalty for my sins.

I invite you to come into my life and make me a part of the family of God.

Come into my life and take control of it.

Thank you for your gift of eternal life and for your Holy Spirit who has come to live in me.

I ask this in Jesus name.

Amen

If you just prayed that prayer, well, you may not feel any different, but you are! Your sins have been forgiven, and you have become a child of God. Jesus promises that anyone who believes in him has become a new creation, the old life has gone and new life has begun. He promises to never leave you nor forsake you. This is the most important invitation you have ever accepted in your life and I pray you will let someone know about it! Find a Christian friend or family member and tell them. If you have a Bible, the Gospel of John is a great place to start to learn more about Jesus and his love for you. If you don't have a Bible, you can go to BibleGateway.com or BibleStudyTools.com and read one online for free.

QUESTIONS TO CONSIDER

Have you made Jesus, the Son of God, who is fully man and fully God, your personal Lord and Savior? If so, remember how you came to make that decision and take a minute to thank Jesus for redeeming you. If you have not yet accepted Jesus as your Savior, what is keeping you from taking that step?

Doubts are a normal part of the spiritual life. Many great saints and disciples struggled with them. Do you ever find yourself struggling with doubts in your spiritual journey? If so, how do you deal with them?

What does the empty tomb mean to you personally? Does the magnitude of Jesus' love for you cause you to live life differently?

RSVP
take time to tell Jesus how you will respond to his invitation

YOU ARE
INVITED
TO SEEK ME

Jesus

AND YOU SHALL
SEEK ME, AND
FIND ME, WHEN
YOU SEARCH FOR
ME WITH ALL
YOUR HEART.

JEREMIAH 29:13

The Beginning, Not the End

Jesus never stops inviting us to draw near, to trust him, to follow him. His love for us knows no bounds and even though we may decline his invitations, or postpone accepting them, he continues to invite us.

That is why this is the beginning, not the end. Every second of every day is a new opportunity to reach out and take the invitation from the hand of the One who loves you, who created you, and who wants to have a relationship with you.

> When Jesus calls and invites you to dine,
> Drop everything and with Him recline.

It is my deepest prayer that the time you have spent reading this devotional and journaling has brought you closer to Jesus. But I also hope that you continue to find ways to draw near to him. Read the Bible, his love letter to you. Journal. Sit in silence, listening for his voice. Walk in his creation and marvel at his goodness.

It is Jesus who is inviting you to draw near. Will you accept?

Dear Lord,

Please continue to reveal yourself to me in powerful ways. Help me to see Your invitations when they are placed before me. Holy Spirit, spur in me the desire to draw near to the Lord. Thank you for your promise to draw near to me. I love you. I praise you. I thank you for all the blessings you have bestowed on me and those that are still to come. I pray this in the precious name of Jesus, the one who invites me. Amen.

About the Author

Lynne Ann Leite is affectionately known as the CurlyGirl4God. A quick look at her driver's license will reveal she is too old to be a girl. But she still sees herself as God's girl, so best to just let her slide on that one.

Lynne is passionate about her faith and family. She is a writer, speaker, but above all, a storyteller. As a child, she lived within walking distance of a public library, and that is when her love of stories began.

Lynne's imagination knows no bounds and has gotten her into a pickle more than once. Now she is putting those crazy ideas to good use to entertain and inspire her readers. Her motto is, "Life is a series of stories meant to be told." Those stories make their way into all her writing. Whether as personal essays for Chicken Soup for the Soul, or in her fiction and non-fiction books.

Most recently, she has married story with poetry in this poetry devotional. Her fourth-grade teacher would be proud, and should feel a little prophetic, since he gave her the title of Class Poet.

Lynne is a speaker for Christian women's events. She has been a speaker for Stonecroft Ministries for many years and now helps new speakers prepare to share their stories for God's glory. A longtime Toastmaster, Lynne has earned the designation of Distinguished Toastmaster.

When Lynne is not writing or lost in her imagination, she loves to watch the butterflies and hummingbirds enjoy her native garden. She lives in Southern California with her husband and uses the area where she lives as the setting for many of her stories. Most of all, she loves spending time with her adult children and being Nana to her grandchildren. They always inspires her to see the world through the eyes of a child. And that's the best inspiration for any storyteller!

You can connect with Lynne online at www.LynneLeite.com.